FORWARD/COMMENTARY

The National Institute of Standards and Technology (NIST) is a measurement standards laboratory, and a non-regulatory agency of the United States Department of Commerce. Its mission is to promote innovation and industrial competitiveness. Founded in 1901, as the National Bureau of Standards, NIST was formed with the mandate to provide standard weights and measures, and to serve as the national physical laboratory for the United States. With a world-class measurement and testing laboratory encompassing a wide range of areas of computer science, mathematics, statistics, and systems engineering, NIST's cybersecurity program supports its overall mission to promote U.S. innovation and industrial competitiveness by advancing measurement science, standards, and related technology through research and development in ways that enhance economic security and improve our quality of life.

The need for cybersecurity standards and best practices that address interoperability, usability and privacy has been shown to be critical for the nation. NIST's cybersecurity programs seek to enable greater development and application of practical, innovative security technologies and methodologies that enhance the country's ability to address current and future computer and information security challenges.

The cybersecurity publications produced by NIST cover a wide range of cybersecurity concepts that are carefully designed to work together to produce a holistic approach to cybersecurity primarily for government agencies and constitute the best practices used by industry. This holistic strategy to cybersecurity covers the gamut of security subjects from development of secure encryption standards for communication and storage of information while at rest, to how best to recover from a cyber-attack.

Why buy a book you can download for free? We print these books so you don't have to.

Some books are available only in electronic media and you need a hard copy. So, you have to print it yourself – not always easy when you share a LAN printer with 100 other people.

We at 4th Watch Books are former government employees, so we know how people actually use these standards. When a new standard is released, an engineer prints it out, punches holes and puts it in a 3-ring binder. While this is not a big deal for a 5 or 10-page document, many work documents are over 100 pages and printing a large document is a time-consuming effort. An engineer that's paid $75 an hour could spend hours simply printing out the tools needed to do the job. That's time that could be better spent doing engineering. We publish these documents so engineers can focus on what they were hired to do – engineering. It's much more cost-effective to simply order the latest version from Amazon.com. If you like the service we provide, please leave positive review on Amazon so we can continue to print books you need. If there is a standard you would like to see printed, let us know. Our web site is Cybah.webplus.net

See a list of all the docs we print on our CyberSecurity Standards Library™ DVD.

1

DRAFT NISTIR 8170

The Cybersecurity Framework

2

Implementation Guidance for Federal Agencies

3

4
5 Matt Barrett
6 Jeff Marron
7 Victoria Yan Pillitteri
8 Jon Boyens
9 Greg Witte
10 Larry Feldman
11

National Institute of Standards and Technology
U.S. Department of Commerce

DRAFT NISTIR 8170

The Cybersecurity Framework

Implementation Guidance for Federal Agencies

Matt Barrett
Jeff Marron
Applied Cybersecurity Division
Information Technology Laboratory

Victoria Yan Pillitteri
Jon Boyens
Computer Security Division
Information Technology Laboratory

Greg Witte
Larry Feldman
G2 Inc.
Annapolis Junction, Maryland

May 2017

U.S. Department of Commerce
Wilbur L. Ross, Jr., Secretary

National Institute of Standards and Technology
Kent Rochford, Acting NIST Director and Under Secretary of Commerce for Standards and Technology

National Institute of Standards and Technology Interagency Report 8170
41 pages (May 2017)

Public comment period: *May 12, 2017* through *June 30, 2017*

National Institute of Standards and Technology
Attn: Applied Cybersecurity Division, Information Technology Laboratory
100 Bureau Drive (Mail Stop 2000) Gaithersburg, MD 20899-2000
Email: nistir8170@nist.gov

All comments are subject to release under the Freedom of Information Act (FOIA).

69
Reports on Computer Systems Technology

70 The Information Technology Laboratory (ITL) at the National Institute of Standards and
71 Technology (NIST) promotes the U.S. economy and public welfare by providing technical
72 leadership for the Nation's measurement and standards infrastructure. ITL develops tests, test
73 methods, reference data, proof of concept implementations, and technical analyses to advance
74 the development and productive use of information technology. ITL's responsibilities include the
75 development of management, administrative, technical, and physical standards and guidelines for
76 the cost-effective security and privacy of other than national security-related information in
77 federal information systems.

78
Acknowledgments

79 The authors would like to thank our advisors and reviewers including Donna Dodson, Adam
80 Sedgewick, Matt Scholl, Kevin Stine, Kelley Dempsey, Ron Ross, Steve Quinn, Jim Foti, Mat
81 Heyman, and Matt Smith.

82
Abstract

83 This publication assists federal agencies in strengthening their cybersecurity risk management by
84 helping them to determine an appropriate implementation of the *Framework for Improving*
85 *Critical Infrastructure Cybersecurity* (known as the Cybersecurity Framework). Federal agencies
86 can use the Cybersecurity Framework to complement the existing suite of NIST security and
87 privacy risk management standards, guidelines, and practices developed in response to the
88 Federal Information Security Management Act, as amended (FISMA). The relationship between
89 the Cybersecurity Framework and the National Institute of Standards and Technology (NIST)
90 Risk Management Framework are discussed in eight use cases.

91
Keywords

92 Cybersecurity Framework; Federal Information Security Management Act (FISMA); Risk
93 Management Framework (RMF); security and privacy controls

94
Supplemental Content

95 For additional information on NIST's cybersecurity programs, projects and publications, visit the
96 Computer Security Resource Center, csrc.nist.gov. Information on other efforts at NIST and in
97 the Information Technology Laboratory (ITL) is available at www.nist.gov and www.nist.gov/itl.

98

99

Note to Reviewers

This document provides guidance on how the *Framework for Improving Critical Infrastructure Cybersecurity* (Cybersecurity Framework) can be used in the U.S. federal government in conjunction with the current and planned suite of NIST security and privacy risk management publications. The specific guidance was derived from current Cybersecurity Framework use.[1] To provide federal agencies with examples of how the Cybersecurity Framework can augment the current versions of NIST security and privacy risk management publications, this guidance uses common federal information security vocabulary and processes.[2] NIST will engage with agencies to add content based on agency implementation, refine current guidance and identify additional guidance to provide the information that is most helpful to agencies. Feedback will also help to determine which Cybersecurity Framework concepts are incorporated into future versions of the suite of NIST security and privacy risk management publications. NIST would like feedback that addresses the following questions:

- How can agencies use the Cybersecurity Framework, and what are the potential opportunities and challenges?

- How does the guidance presented in this draft report benefit federal agency cybersecurity risk management?

- How does the draft report help stakeholders to better understand federal agency use of the Cybersecurity Framework?

- How does the draft report inform potential updates to the suite of NIST security and privacy risk management publications to promote an integrated approach to risk management?

- Which documents among the suite of NIST security and privacy risk management publications should incorporate Cybersecurity Framework concepts, and where?

- How can this report be improved to provide better guidance to federal agencies?

Conventions

The phrase "federal agencies" in this publication means those agencies responsible for non-national security-related information in federal systems.

FISMA refers to the Federal Information Security Management Act of 2002, as amended.[3]

"Cybersecurity Framework" refers to version 1.0 of the *"Framework for Improving Critical Infrastructure Cybersecurity*, issued in February 2014."[4]

---

[1] Such as use of the Industry Resources located at the Cybersecurity Framework Web site:
https://www.nist.gov/cyberframework/industry-resources

[2] The suite of NIST security and privacy risk management publications include: Federal Information Processing Standards (FIPS) Publication 199, FIPS Publication 200, Special Publication (SP) 800-53, SP 800-37, SP 800-137, SP 800-39, and SP 800-30.

[3] *The Federal Information Security Management Act of 2002* was updated through the *Federal Information Security Modernization Act of 2014.*

[4] The *Framework for Improving Critical Infrastructure Cybersecurity* is found at: https://www.nist.gov/cyberframework

132 The term "Tiers" cited in NIST Special Publication 800-39, *Managing Information Security*
133 *Risk: Organization, Mission, and Information System View*, will be referred to as "Levels" in this
134 report to avoid confusion with Cybersecurity Framework Implementation Tiers.

135 The six steps of the Risk Management Framework described in NIST Special Publication 800-
136 37, *Guide for Applying the Risk Management Framework to Federal Information Systems: A*
137 *Security Life Cycle Approach* – Categorize, Select, Implement, Assess, Authorize, and Monitor –
138 are indicated using capital letters. This includes all conjugations (e.g., Authorize, Authorizing,
139 and Authorized all refer to step five of the RMF).

140 The five Functions of the Cybersecurity Framework – Identify, Protect, Detect, Respond, and
141 Recover – are indicated using capital letters. This includes all conjugations (e.g., Detect,
142 Detected, and Detecting all refer to the Detect Function of Cybersecurity Framework).

143 The terms "enterprise risk management" and "organization-wide risk management" are used
144 interchangeably.
145

146 **Executive Summary**

147   All federal agencies are charged and entrusted with safeguarding the information that is
148   contained in their systems and with ensuring that these systems operate securely and reliably. In
149   a world where cyber systems are constantly challenged by more frequent and often more creative
150   and sophisticated attacks, it is vital that agency personnel – from the most senior executives to
151   line staff – manage their assets and cybersecurity risks wisely. To do that well, they need the
152   most capable, up-to-date, and easy-to-use approaches and tools, including a holistic approach to
153   risk management.

154   The National Institute of Standards and Technology (NIST) is responsible for developing
155   standards and guidelines – including minimum requirements – to provide adequate information
156   security for federal information and information systems. This suite of security and privacy risk
157   management standards and guidelines provides guidance for an integrated, organization-wide
158   program to manage information security risk. In response to a new executive order issued by the
159   President on May 11, 2017 and as part of its initiative to continuously improve the risk
160   management resources provided to federal agencies, NIST has produced this report providing
161   federal agencies with guidance on how the *Framework for Improving Critical Infrastructure*
162   *Cybersecurity* (known as the Cybersecurity Framework) can help agencies to complement
163   existing risk management practices and improve their cybersecurity risk management programs.

164   Developed by NIST in 2013-2014 working closely with the private and public sectors, the
165   Cybersecurity Framework is a risk management approach used voluntarily by organizations
166   across the United States. It also is receiving attention in other countries and regions around the
167   world. Prepared initially to address cybersecurity challenges in the nation's critical infrastructure
168   sectors, the voluntary Framework aligns with and complements the suite of NIST security and
169   privacy risk management standards and guidelines.

170   This report illustrates eight use cases in which federal agencies can leverage the Cybersecurity
171   Framework to address common cybersecurity-related responsibilities. By doing so, agencies can
172   seamlessly integrate the Cybersecurity Framework with key NIST cybersecurity risk
173   management standards and guidelines already in wide use at various organizational levels. The
174   result will be a more robust and mature agency-wide cybersecurity risk management program.
175   The eight use cases are:

176   1. *Integrate Enterprise and Cybersecurity Risk Management*
177   2. *Manage Cybersecurity Requirements*
178   3. *Integrate and Align Cybersecurity and Acquisition Processes*
179   4. *Evaluate Organizational Cybersecurity*
180   5. *Manage the Cybersecurity Program*
181   6. *Maintain a Comprehensive Understanding of Cybersecurity Risk*
182   7. *Report Cybersecurity Risks*
183   8. *Inform the Tailoring Process*

184   The key concepts of the Cybersecurity Framework and the proposed federal cybersecurity uses
185   described in this document are intended to promote the dialog with federal agencies. This will
186   inform near-term updates to the suite of applicable NIST cybersecurity and privacy risk
187   management publications, including updates to Special Publications 800-37 and 800-53.
188   Recognizing the importance of clear, timely guidance to assist agencies in carrying out their

189 cybersecurity-related responsibilities, NIST will use federal agency feedback to inform and
190 prioritize accelerated updates of those documents.

191 **Table of Contents**

220

221 **1   Introduction**

222 As part of its statutory responsibilities under the Federal Information Security Management Act
223 as amended (FISMA), NIST develops standards and guidelines – including minimum
224 requirements – to provide adequate information security for all agency operations and assets.
225 Fulfilling the requirements of FISMA and OMB Circular A-130[5], these documents include
226 Federal Information Processing Standards (FIPS), Special Publications (SPs), and NIST
227 Interagency Reports (NISTIRs), which are used by agencies to develop, implement, and maintain
228 cybersecurity and privacy programs

229 The Cybersecurity Enhancement Act of 2014 formally updated NIST's role to include
230 identifying and developing cybersecurity risk frameworks for voluntary use by critical
231 infrastructure (CI) owners and operators. That statute's assignments included work NIST had
232 begun in February 2013 as a result of Executive Order (EO) 13636, *Improving Critical*
233 *Infrastructure Cybersecurity.*[6] The EO tasked the Department of Commerce to lead the
234 development of a framework to reduce CI cybersecurity risks. NIST convened industry,
235 academia, and government to develop a voluntary *Framework for Improving Critical*
236 *Infrastructure Cybersecurity* (known as the Cybersecurity Framework) that consists of standards,
237 methodologies, procedures, and processes that align policy, business, and technological
238 approaches to address cybersecurity risks. It offers a high-level vocabulary for cybersecurity risk
239 management, a taxonomy of cybersecurity outcomes, and a methodology to assess and manage
240 those outcomes.

241 The increasing frequency, creativity, and variety of cyber attacks means that a greater emphasis
242 must be placed by all organizations on managing cybersecurity risk as a part of their enterprise
243 risk management programs to fulfill their mission and business objectives. By seamlessly
244 integrating the Cybersecurity Framework and key NIST cybersecurity risk management
245 standards and guidelines already in wide use at various organizational levels, agencies can
246 develop, implement, and continuously improve agency-wide cybersecurity risk management
247 processes that inform strategic, operational, and other enterprise risk decisions.[7]

248 *1.1 Audience*

249 This document is intended for those who are responsible for overseeing, leading, and managing
250 information systems within their agencies. That includes senior executives and line managers
251 and staff – and every level in between. It is especially relevant for personnel who develop,

---

[5] https://www.federalregister.gov/documents/2016/07/28/2016-17872/revision-of-omb-circular-no-a-130-managing-information-
as-a-strategic-resource
[6] https://www.federalregister.gov/documents/2013/02/19/2013-03915/improving-critical-infrastructure-cybersecurity
[7] While this report is intended to help federal agencies to incorporate key Cybersecurity Framework elements into their
programs, *publication of this document will not affect the Cybersecurity Framework's primary focus on private sector critical
infrastructure owners and operators.*

252 implement, report, and improve enterprise and cybersecurity risk management processes within
253 their organizations. While the focus is on federal users, NIST expects that many public and
254 private sector organizations that choose to use the NIST cybersecurity risk management suite of
255 standards and guidelines will benefit from this document, including the use cases that are
256 presented.

257 *1.2 Organization of this Report*

258 The remainder of this document is structured as follows:

259 • Section 2 provides guidance that includes eight descriptions of how federal agencies can
260   effectively use the Cybersecurity Framework in conjunction with existing NIST standards
261   and guidelines to develop, implement, and continuously improve their cybersecurity risk
262   management programs.
263 • Section 3 describes plans for an integrated federal approach to cybersecurity risk
264   management.
265 • Appendix A summarizes NIST cybersecurity risk management standards and guidelines.
266 • Appendix B lists and explains acronyms that appear in the document.
267 • Appendix C defines key terms.
268 • Appendix D lists references with additional information.

269 **2   Guidance**

270   Using eight common government cybersecurity needs, this section provides guidance that can
271   assist federal agencies as they develop, implement, and continuously improve their cybersecurity
272   risk management programs. It is consistent with OMB's policy guidance to federal agencies
273   contained in OMB Circular A-130, *Managing Information as a Strategic Resource.* That circular
274   provides guidance regarding the Risk Management Framework (described in NIST SP 800-37),
275   associated documents, and the Cybersecurity Framework.

---

276   **OMB Circular A-130 Appendix I, Section 5.q**

277   **Responsibiities for Protecting and Managing Federal Information Resources**

278   *The [Cybersecurity] Framework is not intended to duplicate the current information security*
279   *and risk management practices in place within the Federal Government. However, in the*
280   *course of managing information security risk using the established NIST Risk Management*
281   *Framework and associated security standards and guidelines required by FISMA, agencies*
282   *can leverage the Cybersecurity Framework to complement their current information security*
283   *programs.*

---

284   NIST will work with federal agencies to assess the relative value of these eight proposed uses,
285   identify additional uses, and understand how to better illustrate applications of the Cybersecurity
286   Framework. The feedback received will guide and inform NIST as it incorporates Cybersecurity
287   Framework concepts into its various cybersecurity risk management publications. These uses
288   illustrate how agencies can leverage both the Cybersecurity Framework and the NIST Risk
289   Management Framework to:

290   • Measure and improve cybersecurity performance at various organizational levels;

291   • Organize communication about cybersecurity risk, activities, and results across the
292   organization-wide risk management program; and

293   • Align and prioritize cybersecurity requirements for use in the acquisition process and to
294   inform the tailoring of controls.

295   Figure 1 depicts federal cybersecurity risk management needs (middle column) superimposed on
296   the three-level pyramid found in one of the primary NIST cybersecurity documents used by
297   federal agencies – *Managing Information Security Risk: Organization, Mission, and Information*
298   *System View* (SP 800-39). Most of the uses addressed in this publication fit in the
299   "Mission/Business Processes" (Level 2). One use is offered that illustrates the "Organization"
300   function (Level 1) and another addresses the "System" (Level 3). In the right column, Figure 1
301   also depicts the most applicable Cybersecurity Framework component – Core, Profile(s), or
302   Implementation Tiers – for a given federal use.

Special Publication 800-39			Cybersecurity Framework Components
	Level 1 Organization	**Integrate enterprise and cybersecurity risk management** by communicating with universally understood risk terms.	Core
		Manage cybersecurity requirements using a construct that enables integration and prioritization of *all* requirements.	Profile(s)
		Integrate and align cybersecurity and acquisition processes by relaying cybersecurity requirements and priorities in a common and concise language	Profile(s)
	Level 2 Mission/ Business Processes	**Evaluate organizational cybersecurity** using a standardized and straightforward measurement scale and set of self-assessment criteria.	Implementation Tiers
		Manage the cybersecurity program by determining which cybersecurity outcomes necessitate common controls, and apportioning work and responsibility for those cybersecurity outcomes (supports RMF Implement & Monitor).	Profile(s)
		Maintain a comprehensive understanding of cybersecurity risk using a standardized organizing structure (supports RMF Authorize).	Core
		Report cybersecurity risks using a universal and understandable reporting structure.	Core
	Level 3 System	**Inform the tailoring process** using a comprehensive reconciliation of *all* cybersecurity requirements (supports RMF Implement).	Profile(s)

303
304

Figure 1: Federal Cybersecurity Uses

305 Federal agencies may determine additional ways the integrated federal approach can or should
306 enhance their cybersecurity risk management programs. NIST intends to develop additional
307 examples of uses based in part on feedback from federal agencies.

308 *1. Integrate Enterprise and Cybersecurity Risk Management*

309 Organizations manage many types of risk and develop specific policies to identify, assess, and
310 help mitigate adverse effects across a wide range of risks, with cybersecurity among them. Some
311 of the other typical risks include: safety, operations, financial, program, acquisitions, customer
312 interactions, supply chain, and privacy. Some of these areas employ different terminologies and
313 risk management approaches to make decisions within the risk area and across the organization
314 as part of an enterprise-wide management process. The Cybersecurity Framework provides
315 organizations the ability to leverage a common language that reaches beyond cybersecurity and
316 across the organization, while allowing these other risk management disciplines to incorporate
317 the Framework's terms or to continue using existing processes.

318 More specifically, the Cybersecurity Framework Core's five "Functions" offer a way to organize
319 cybersecurity risk management activities at their highest levels using words that can be applied
320 across risk management disciplines: Identify, Protect, Detect, Respond, and Recover. Many
321 stakeholders from varied parts of an organization can understand and already use these five
322 words in the context of risk decisions. While the Cybersecurity Framework links them to
323 specific cybersecurity outcomes, other disciplines heavily dependent on risk management such as

324   finance and physical security may choose to integrate their unique processes and terminologies
325   into the Framework's Functions to facilitate communication.

326   For example, CISOs and other cybersecurity professionals in federal agencies can use these five
327   Functions as a way to engage, organize and explain their cybersecurity approaches to agency
328   external stakeholders, executive leadership, and employees and to integrate cybersecurity
329   concepts into other organizational areas. The Functions provide an understandable and intuitive
330   language for CISOs to gather risk tolerance perspectives from their peers and leadership team.
331   The Functions are also a simple way to organize and express a risk strategy to address those risk
332   tolerances. This helps CISOs to collaborate with stakeholders from various parts of the
333   organization (e.g. human resources, finance, legal, acquisition) in identifying common priorities
334   and assets and the risk-based strategies to address those common priorities. When representatives
335   across an organization are engaged and instrumental in identifying and prioritizing
336   organizational assets and determining risk management strategies, the results are more likely to
337   achieve the desired outcomes.

338   *Integrate Enterprise and Cybersecurity Risk Management*

Benefit(s): • Facilitate communication, • Provide common language that reaches beyond cybersecurity risk management and encompasses other risk management disciplines.	**Primary SP 800-39 Level:** 1 - Organization
	Primary Cybersecurity Framework Component: Core
Summary: Using the Cybersecurity Framework's Functions (Identify, Protect, Detect, Respond, and Recover) as the basis for risk management dialogs, organizations can raise awareness of cybersecurity and other risks to be managed and facilitate communication among agency stakeholders, including executive leadership.[8] This is enabled when other disciplines participating in the enterprise risk management dialog link their existing approaches to the Functions. This Use example aggregates the activities of Uses 2-8.	
Typical Participants: Head of Agency (Chief Executive Officer), Risk Executive (Function), Chief Information Officer, Senior Information Security Officer/Chief Information Security Officer (CISO), stakeholders representing other risk management disciplines (e.g., Finance, Human Resources, Acquisition).	
Primary NIST Documents: NIST Special Publication 800-39, Cybersecurity Framework	

339   *2. Manage Cybersecurity Requirements*

340   Federal agencies, like private sector organizations, are subject to multiple cybersecurity
341   requirements. For agencies, these may include (but are not limited to) laws, regulations,
342   oversight by and reports to Congress, internal policy, and Office of Management and Budget
343   policies. The Cybersecurity Framework can be used by federal agencies for requirements
344   management through the process of integration and prioritization.

---

[8] Source: OMB A-130

345 Agencies can integrate requirements by aligning and de-conflicting using the structure of the
346 Core. For instance, a federal agency may need to abide by FISMA, the Health Insurance
347 Portability and Accountability Act (HIPAA) Security Rule, the Payment Card Industry Data
348 Security Standard, as well as their own cybersecurity policy, all while accomplishing a mission
349 objective. Applicable excerpts of these laws, guidelines, policy, and objectives can be aligned
350 with the various Functions, Categories, and Subcategores of the Core. By reconciling
351 cybersecurity requirements in this manner, a federal agency can determine where requirements
352 overlap and/or conflict, and consider alternative approaches, perhaps including modification of
353 cybersecurity requirements in that agency's control, to address those requirements. In turn, this
354 offers the agency the opportunity to improve its efficiency as well as its effectiveness.

355 By integrating requirements into the Core, agencies stage efficient prioritization. For instance, it
356 may be apparent that certain Subcategory outcomes are meaningful for multiple requirements. It
357 may also be clear that a short list of Subcategories are essential for successful achievement of
358 mission objectives. Priorities can be captured in the structure of the Core and used as inputs to
359 drive cybersecurity investments, effort, and focus.

360 The work product of cybersecurity requirements management using Cybersecurity Framework is
361 referred to as a Profile. See Appendix A for additional description and uses of Cybersecurity
362 Framework Profiles.

363 *Manage Cybersecurity Requirements*

Benefit(s):	Primary SP 800-39 Level:
• Determine where cybersecurity requirements overlap and/or conflict in order to ensure compliance and improve efficiency and effectiveness.	2 – Mission/Business Processes
• Prioritize Subcategory outcomes based on the reconciliation of requirements, as well as mission priorities and the operational environment/threat information. • Operationalize cybersecurity activities based on the Cybersecurity Framework Profile.	**Primary Cybersecurity Framework Components:** Core, Profile(s)

Summary: Federal agencies can use the Cybersecurity Framework Core Subcategories to align and de-conflict cybersecurity requirements applicable to their organizations. This reconciliation of requirements helps to ensure compliance and provides input in prioritizing requirements across the organization using the subcategory outcomes. This becomes a means of operationalizing cybersecurity activities and a tool for iterative, dynamic, and prioritized risk management for the agency.
Typical Participants: Risk Executive, Chief Information Officer, Senior Information Security Officer/Chief Information Security Officer (CISO)
Primary NIST Documents: NIST Special Publication 800-39, Cybersecurity Framework

364   *3. Integrate and Align Cybersecurity and Acquisition Processes*

365   Federal agencies and contractors must adhere to both common and unique cybersecurity and
366   acquisition requirements[9]. In the acquisition process, this often causes a misunderstanding of
367   expectations between federal agencies and offerors and may limit government access to the best
368   products and services, while increasing costs to offerors, agencies, and taxpayers.

369   The Cybersecurity Framework can be used to translate among a variety of risk management
370   practices and support federal agencies as they interact with a wide variety of suppliers. These
371   include service providers, product vendors, systems integrators, organizations within a regulated
372   sector, and other private sector partners.

373   For example, an agency could use the Cybersecurity Framework during market research by
374   asking respondents to a Request For Information or Sources Sought Notice to include their
375   Cybersecurity Framework Profile or to express the cybersecurity capabilities of their product in
376   responses. This information would help the agency to better compare and contrast the
377   cybersecurity capabilities of organizations, products and services of respondents.

378   By using Profiles, the Cybersecurity Framework can be incorporated into the acquisition process
379   as the underpinning of: evaluation criteria (agency), solicitation response (supplier),
380   proposal/quote review (agency), minimum contract requirements (agency), contract compliance
381   evidence (supplier), and contract compliance verification (agency). The use of Profiles allows
382   suppliers the flexibility to select from among various standards and practices to meet federal
383   agency specific requirements, while communicating their cybersecurity posture in a consistent
384   way. It also provides agencies a means to consistently and objectively assess the cybersecurity
385   posture of potential partners.

386   *Integrate and Align Cybersecurity and Acquisition Processes*

Benefit(s):	Primary SP 800-39 Level:
<ul><li>Ability to determine which cybersecurity standards and practices to incorporate into contracts.</li></ul>	2 – Mission/Business Processes
<ul><li>Provides a common language to communicate requirements to offerors and awardees (agreement/contract)</li><li>Allows offerors to express their cybersecurity posture and related standards and practices.</li></ul>	**Primary Cybersecurity Framework Component:** Profile(s)

Summary: For acquisitions that present cybersecurity risks, federal agencies can choose to do business with organizations that meet minimum cybersecurity requirements in their operations and in the products and services they deliver. Cybersecurity Framework Profiles can be used by federal agencies to express technical requirements; offerors can demonstrate how they meet or exceed these requirements.
Typical Participants: Risk Executive (Function), Chief Information Officer, Senior Information Security Officer/Chief Information Security Officer (CISO), General Counsel, Contracting Office, Mission/Business owner
Primary NIST Documents: NIST Special Publications 800-39, 800-161, 800-171, Cybersecurity Framework

---

[9] Compare, e.g., FAR § 52.204-21, *Basic Safeguarding of Covered Contractor Information System*s (common), with DFARS 252.204-7012 *Safeguarding Covered Defense Information and Cyber Incident Reporting* (unique), and OMB Circular No. A-130, *Managing Information as a Strategic Resource* (common), with DoD Instruction 8500.01, *Cybersecurity* (unique).

387 *4. Evaluate Organizational Cybersecurity*

388 The Implementation Tiers are designed as an overarching measurement of cybersecurity risk
389 management behaviors within an organization. They help an organization to consider the
390 maturity of each of the following cybersecurity properties on a scale from 1-4 (Partial, Risk
391 Informed, Repeatable, and Adaptive):

- 392 • Risk Management Process - Does our organization have a cybersecurity risk management
  393 process that is functioning and repeatable?

- 394 • Integrated Risk Management Program – To what extent is cybersecurity risk management
  395 integrated into enterprise risk management?

- 396 • External Participation – To what degree is our organization (or units within the
  397 organization) sharing with and receiving cybersecurity information from outside parties?

398 Unlike some maturity models, the Implementation Tiers are not prescriptive. In other words,
399 there is no set requirement for an organization and all of its sub-organizations to operate at
400 Implementation Tier 4. Rather, Implementation Tiers can be used for informed trade-off
401 analysis, since there is a corresponding cost and risk tolerance associated with each
402 Implementation Tier. For example, to balance finite resources across all agency cybersecurity
403 considerations, it may be appropriate to operate at Implementation Tier 2 in one part of an
404 agency in order to afford to operate at Implementation Tier 4 elsewhere. One way that federal
405 agencies may apply these trade-offs is via FIPS-199 categorizations. An agency might view
406 FIPS-199 High Impact and High Value Asset[10] (HVA) systems as appropriate for higher
407 Implementation Tiers. Conversely, the agency may determine that operating at a lower
408 Implementation Tier for FIPS-199 Low Impact categorized systems is acceptable.

409 Agencies can evaluate the Implementation Tier at which they are operating in comparison to the
410 desired Tier. This process may identify gaps between the current and the target Implementation
411 Tier, as well as steps that the organization can take to progress to a desired Tier. These gaps
412 indicate there is a difference between current and optimal cybersecurity risk management
413 behaviors. Agency Implementation Tier targets may be influenced by external requiremnts,
414 including OMB policies and OMB cross-agency priorities.

415 *Evaluate Organizational Cybersecurity*

Benefit(s): • Assist agencies in critically evaluating their cybersecurity risk management behaviors and identifying opportunities for improvement. • Enable agencies to make informed trade-offs concerning the appropriateness of and investments in the cybersecurity of particular organizational units or systems.	**Primary SP 800-39 Level:** 2 – Mission/Business Processes
	Primary Cybersecurity Framework Component: Implementation Tiers
Summary: Implementation Tiers provide agencies a basis for rationalizing different modes of cybersecurity operations across an organization. That is based on trade-off analysis of target Implementation Tiers for various agency business units or specific assets. Gap analysis between the current and Target Implementation Tier will reveal opportunities for prioritizing improvement investments.	

---

[10] High Value Asset as first referenced in OMB Memorandum M-16-04 and defined in M-17-09

Typical Participants: Head of Agency (Chief Executive Officer), Agency Deputy (Chief Operating Officer) Risk Executive, Chief Information Officer, Senior Information Security Officer/Chief Information Security Officer (CISO), stakeholders representing other risk management disciplines (e.g., Finance, Human Resources, Acquisition)

Primary NIST Documents: NIST Special Publication 800-39, Cybersecurity Framework

416 *5. Manage the Cybersecurity Program*

417 The Core taxonomy of cybersecurity outcomes that are captured in subcategories provides a
418 logical structure to organize cybersecurity operations within an agency – specifically, how work
419 gets assigned, tracked, and measured, and how personnel empowerment and accountability is
420 managed.

421 The Cybersecurity Framework provides a way to assign cybersecurity responsibility to units or
422 individuals in an organization. When doing so, executives can specify tasks, responsibilities, and
423 authorities of the cybersecurity program and its associated strategies. This also allows executives
424 to empower units and individuals and to reward them appropriately. If parts of cybersecurity
425 operations are not performing as intended or risk is beyond set threshold levels, the
426 Cybersecurity Framework structure enables managers to trace and investigate the situation and to
427 hold relevant units and individuals accountable.

428 The Cybersecurity Framework provides a manageable way to apportion responsibility for
429 cybersecurity – most importantly for the desired outcomes associated with assigned Core
430 Functions, Categories, or Subcategories. Since controls in SP 800-53 map to the Cybersecurity
431 Framework, responsibility for the corresponding controls can also be assigned to these
432 individuals.

433 When analyzing the desired cybersecurity outcomes associated with Core Categories and
434 Subcategories, certain outcomes may be more cost-effectively managed for the entire agency by
435 one unit rather than by each organizational unit separately. For example, an agency may
436 determine that responsibility for Subcategory PR.AC-2 "Physical access to assets is managed
437 and protected" is most cost-effectively made the responsibility of the Physical Security unit for
438 the benefit of the entire agency. Conversely, the agency may decide that responsibility for the
439 cybersecurity outcomes of other Subcategories is shared between business units and/or systems.
440 These determinations can assist federal agencies in identifying candidate common and hybrid
441 controls as specified in SP 800-53.

442 Another way for federal agencies to identify common cybersecurity controls is by identifying
443 common assets and business processes. Managers of various business units within agencies have
444 a key role in identifying high value assets and business processes. The ensuing discussions
445 among the business unit managers, CISO, and other stakeholders of how to prioritize and protect
446 these assets will likely indicate business units which have similar assets or business processes
447 and which can utilize shared services to protect these high value assets. That can logically lead to

448 the identification of common controls to secure assets and business processes across business
449 units. It also can yield significant cost savings.

450 *Manage the Cybersecurity Program*

Benefit(s):	Primary SP 800-39 Level:
• Provide a way to apportion responsibility and authority for cybersecurity outcomes to business units and/or individuals using the Core. • Provide a way to empower, reward, and hold accountable units and individuals charged with certain cybersecurity responsibilities. • Identify common controls and hybrid controls via analysis of the cybersecurity outcomes in the Core and apportion responsibility for these outcomes to business units and/or individuals. • Save significant resources by identifying common controls.	2 – Business/Mission Processes **Primary Cybersecurity Framework Component:** Core

Summary: The Core taxonomy of cybersecurity outcomes in Subcategories provides a way to apportion responsibility for these cybersecurity outcomes to organizational business units or individuals. Analysis of the cybersecurity outcomes in the Cybersecurity Framework Core also can assist agencies in identifying common and hybrid controls and saving resources.

Typical Participants: Chief Information Officer, Senior Information Security Officer/Chief Information Security Officer (CISO), Common Control Provider

Primary NIST Documents: NIST Special Publication 800-37, Cybersecurity Framework

451
452 *6. Maintain a Comprehensive Understanding of Cybersecurity Risk*

453 By aggregating cybersecurity findings, gaps and vulnerabilities into a centralized record,
454 agencies can gain a single view of cybersecurity risk at an aggregate level. That understanding
455 can better inform risk decisions. Examples include determining how a system Authorization
456 decision might affect the agency as a whole or how broader risk decisions might play out in a
457 complex and connected infrastructure. An organization-wide record of risk will also enable
458 consistent reporting. In some organizations, this centralized record is referred to as a "risk
459 register."

460 Agencies currently track managed vulnerabilities, vulnerability mitigation plans, and accepted
461 vulnerabilities on a system-by-system basis. This information is in the system Security
462 Authorization Package, which includes the system security plan (SSP), the security assessment
463 report (SAR), and the plan of action and milestones (POA&Ms)[11]. Through these artifacts,
464 agencies: track planned security and privacy controls, assess the implementation of controls,
465 annotate weaknesses or deficiencies in security controls, identify residual vulnerabilities in the
466 system, and highlight mitigation plans. The information in these key documents is used by
467 Authorizing Officials (AO) to make risk-based Authorization decisions.

468 Using the Cybersecurity Framework, an organization can assemble system-level weaknesses or
469 deficiencies into an enterprise-wide understanding of cybersecurity vulnerabilities. Including

---
[11] Security Authorization artifacts and process detailed in SP 800-37rev1 Appendix F

17

470 weaknesses or deficiencies across the enterprise can provide a comprehensive understanding of
471 vulnerabilities and planned mitigations. This information can be viewed at the Subcategory,
472 Category, or Function level to provide agencies additional context before making risk decisions
473 and associated resource investments.

474 Further, aggregating essential information from SARs, POA&Ms, and SSPs enables security
475 Authorization decisions through continuous monitoring. Security control assessments,
476 remediation actions, and key updates to the SARs, POA&Ms and SSPs for the system-at-hand
477 can be considered in the context of the organization's aggregate risk. The risk register is also
478 curated using the on-going risk changes tracked through Risk Management Framework (RMF)
479 Monitor activities. The risk register is a tool that helps the AO understand if accepting the system
480 risk will drive overall risk beyond organizational tolerance. Organizing the risk register
481 according to the language of the Core also enables a larger group of people to participate in and
482 inform the Authorization decision. In particular, the understandable language of Functions and
483 Categories of the Core enables non-cybersecurity experts to participate.

484 *Maintain a Comprehensive Understanding of Cybersecurity Risk*

Benefits):	Primary SP 800-39 Level: 2 – Mission/Business Processes
• Assist federal agencies to obtain a better understanding of aggregate risk to enable RMF Authorization decisions.	
	Primary Cybersecurity Framework Component: Core
Summary: The Cybersecurity Framework Core can help agencies to better organize the risks they have accepted and the risks they are working to remediate across all systems. This aggregate and comprehensive understanding of risk enables more informed and effective RMF Authorization decisions.	
Typical Participants: Senior Information Security Officer/Chief Information Security Officer (CISO), Authorizing Official	
Primary NIST Documents: NIST Special Publication 800-37, Cybersecurity Framework	

485 *7. Report Cybersecurity Risks*

486 With the risk register structured according to the Cybersecurity Framework Core, an
487 organization can very efficiently generate risk reports. Reports often need to be distributed to a
488 variety of audiences including: business process personnel, who manage risks as a part of their
489 daily responsibilities; senior executives, who approve and are responsible for agency operations
490 and investment strategies based on risk; other internal units; and external organizations. This
491 means reports need to vary significantly in both transparency and detail, depending on the
492 recipient and report requirement. At the same time, reports need to be clear and understandable.
493 A standardized reporting format can assist agencies in multiple cybersecurity reporting needs

494   Additionally, the timeliness of reports is critical for two reasons. First, reporting needs to match
495   the timeline expectations of the receiving parties. Second, reports often need to represent current
496   state, so the time between risk measurement and report delivery needs to be minimized.

497   Today, risk reporting within federal organizations is performed using a variety of technologies
498   and reporting formats due to different sources requesting information for different purposes and
499   with a high degree of variability in reporting timelines. In recent years, the Office of
500   Management and Budget has requested annual FISMA metrics organized using the structure of
501   the Cybersecurity Framework's Core. With an increasing number of federal organizations,
502   partners, and suppliers using the Cybersecurity Framework, it is more efficient to use the
503   Framework's approach to meet these multiple reporting needs.

504   Structuring a risk register according to the hierarchy of cybersecurity outcomes in the Core
505   allows organizations to generate reports at varying levels of detail. Specifically, relating the
506   hierarchy of five Functions, Categories, and Subcategories to SP 800-53 controls allows
507   maximum flexibility in the level of detail of a given report, and can make those reports more
508   useful to varied audiences. That level of detail can be achieved quickly using the Core,
509   minimizing time and resources invested in generating the report.

510   *Report Cybersecurity Risks*

Benefit(s): • Provide expeditious, audience-appropriate, easy-to-understand, standardized reporting	**Primary SP 800-39 Level:** 2 – Mission/Business Processes
	Primary Cybersecurity Framework Component: Core
Summary: The Cybersecurity Framework Core provides a reporting structure and language that aligns to SP 800-53 controls. This enables easy roll-up of control status into a reporting structure that is appropriate to and understandable by a given audience.	
Typical Participants: Head of Agency (Chief Executive Officer), Deputy Head of Agency (Chief Operating Officer) Risk Executive (Function), Chief Information Officer, Information Owner/Steward, Senior Information Security Officer/Chief Information Security Officer (CISO), stakeholders representing other risk management disciplines (e.g., Finance, Human Resources, Acquisition)	
Primary NIST Documents: NIST Special Publication 800-37rev1, Cybersecurity Framework	

511   *8. Inform the Tailoring Process*

512   Information systems are most valuable when their features explicitly support an organization's
513   mission objectives and requirements.

514   In the RMF, after the system is categorized based on FIPS 199/SP 800-60, organizations
515   leverage FIPS 200 to identify minimum security requirements associated with the system impact
516   level. They then use the SP 800-53 tailoring process to apply any other needed security to
517   address specific mission objectives, operational constraints, cybersecurity requirements, and

518 other organizational considerations. This process is used to customize the controls baseline for
519 each system.

520 The Cybersecurity Framework offers a mechanism for reconciling mission objectives and
521 cybersecurity requirements into Profiles, making them an important work product using a top-
522 down approach to inform the tailoring. In developing a Profile, organizations can align and de-
523 conflict all mission objectives and cybersecurity requirements into a singular structure according
524 to the taxonomy of the Core. That allows organizations to easily prioritize the cybersecurity
525 outcomes of the Subcategories. Since Profiles can be a reconciliation of cybersecurity
526 requirements and associated priorities from many sources, Profiles can be used as a concise and
527 important artifact for consideration when tailoring SP 800-53 initial control baselines to final
528 control baselines. Specifically, considering organizational Subcategory priorities and knowing
529 the associated SP 800-53 controls may lead to precise adjustments to the initial controls baseline
530 in ways that best support the organizational mission.

531 *Inform the Tailoring Process*

Benefit(s): • Provide a single document that reflects mission objectives and applicable agency cybersecurity requirements as a basis for tailoring initial system controls baselines.	**Primary SP 800-39 Level:** 3 - System
	Primary Cybersecurity Framework Component: Profile(s)
Summary: Cybersecurity Framework Profiles enable agencies to reconcile mission objectives and cybersecurity requirements into the structure of the Cybersecurity Framework Core. This readily translates to the SP 800-53 controls that are most meaningful to the organization. Profiles can be used to tailor initial SP 800-53 baselines into final baselines, as deployed in the RMF Implementation step.	
Typical Participants: Information Owner/Steward, Information System Owner, Information Security Architect, Information System Security Engineer, stakeholders representing other risk management disciplines (e.g., Finance, Human Resources, Acquisition)	
Primary NIST Documents: NIST Special Publication 800-53rev4, Cybersecurity Framework	

532

533 **3   Plans for an Integrated Federal Approach**

535 Under FISMA, NIST is clearly assigned to develop and issue "standards [and guidelines] that
536 provide minimum information security requirements," and "improve the efficiency of operation
537 or [the effectiveness of] security of Federal information systems.[12]"

538 As part of those responsibilities, NIST has been leading an initiative to advance and evolve the
539 integrated federal approach to cybersecurity by placing an increased emphasis on risk
540 management. As drivers for this evolution, this initiative:

541   • Uses cybersecurity effectiveness, agency efficiency, and repeatable processes,
542   • Proposes solutions for varied and dynamic federal cybersecurity challenges,
543   • Identifies, validates, and integrates valuable concepts,
544   • Streamlines federal cybersecurity risk management standards and guidelines, and
545   • Relies on OMB A-130 as the primary policy requirement.

546 The key concepts of the Cybersecurity Framework and the federal cybersecurity uses described
547 in this document are intended to promote the dialog with federal agencies. This exchange will
548 inform near-term updates to the suite of affected NIST cybersecurity and privacy risk
549 management publications. Recognizing the importance of clear, timely guidance to assist federal
550 agencies in carrying out their cybersecurity-related responsibilities, NIST will accelerate the
551 update of those documents, beginning with publication of this draft report. As a next step,
552 consistent with NIST's practices, federal agency feedback will be used to inform and prioritize
553 these updates. NIST also may use mechanisms that are more formal in order to gain wider input.
554 These may include the option of issuing a Request for Comment (RFC) or a Request for
555 Information (RFI) for certain elements of the suite of federal standards, guidelines, and
556 publications. NIST will select the most effective and expeditious path forward.

---

[12] https://www.gpo.gov/fdsys/pkg/PLAW-107publ347/pdf/PLAW-107publ347.pdf.

557 **Appendix A—Summary of NIST Risk Management Publications**

558 This appendix describes several NIST cybersecurity risk management publications referenced
559 throughout this document.

560 **Brief Overview of Key Publications**

561 NIST cybersecurity risk management (RM) standards, guidelines and other documents set out
562 RM processes and guide continual improvement of cybersecurity. Three of these are:

- 563 The *Framework for Improving Critical Infrastructure Cybersecurity* (Cybersecurity
  564 Framework)
- 565 NIST SP 800-39, *Managing Information Security Risk: Organization, Mission, and*
  566 *Information System View*
- 567 NIST SP 800-37, *Guide for Applying the Risk Management Framework to Federal*
  568 *Information Systems: A Security Life Cycle Approach*

569 The *Framework for Improving Critical Infrastructure Cybersecurity* (generally referred to as the
570 Cybersecurity Framework) provides a flexible, repeatable and cost effective risk-based approach
571 to implementing security practices. Developed initially for use by critical infrastructure (CI)
572 owners and operators but now used more broadly, the Framework is based on existing standards,
573 guidelines, and practices. It helps an organization to better understand, manage, and reduce its
574 cybersecurity risks and can assist in determining which activities are most important to assure
575 critical operations and service delivery. In turn, that will help to prioritize investments and
576 maximize the impact of each dollar spent on cybersecurity. By providing a common language to
577 address cybersecurity risk management, it is especially helpful in communicating inside and
578 outside the organization. That includes improving communications, awareness, and
579 understanding between and among IT, planning, and operating units, as well as senior
580 executives. Organizations also can readily use the Framework to communicate the current or
581 desired cybersecurity posture between a buyer or supplier.

582 NIST SP 800-39, *Managing Information Security Risk: Organization, Mission, and Information*
583 *System View*, describes a process to manage cybersecurity risk. The process details individual
584 steps to Frame, Assess, Respond, and Monitor cybersecurity risk, in alignment with ISO 31000,
585 31010, 27001, and 27005. The process is supported by descriptions of key high-level
586 cybersecurity risk management roles and responsibilities. Similar to the Cybersecurity
587 Framework, SP 800-39 defines cybersecurity risk management at enterprise, business process,
588 and system levels. The publication is foundational for coordinating those multiple levels of
589 personnel to manage cybersecurity risk.

590 NIST SP 800-37, *Guide for Applying the Risk Management Framework to Federal Information*
591 *Systems: A Security Life Cycle Approach*, details a process to provision secure systems. The six-
592 step Risk Management Framework (RMF) coordinates inter-related risk management standards
593 and guidelines to provision appropriate security controls for a given system. The process shows
594 detailed steps and substeps to implement, authorize, and manage system security controls. The

595 RMF utilizes the SP 800-39 roles to coordinate multiple Levels of personnel to provision secure
596 systems.

Preliminary Guidance Analysis

598 As displayed in Figure 1, the requirements reconciliation process is critical for managing
599 cybersecurity risk. Many cybersecurity requirements originate from mission objectives, laws,
600 regulation, and policy. These must be aligned and deconflicted so that organizational
601 cybersecurity dependencies become apparent. The requirements are then integrated into
602 organizational cybersecurity risk management strategy and supportive activities. Those same
603 requirements inform decision making about provisioning secure systems. Finally, provisioning
604 secure systems is a foundational component to managing cybersecurity risk.

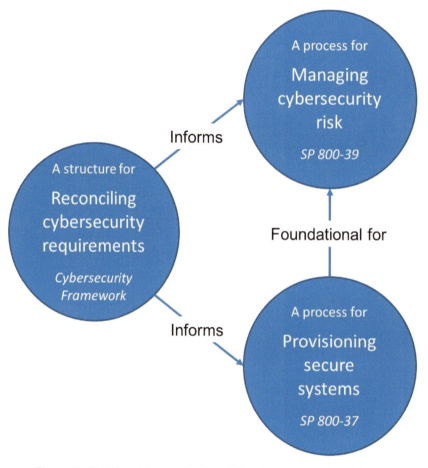

605
606 **Figure 1: Relationships of Key NIST Risk Management Guidance**
607

Basis for Document Alignment

609 The complex relationships among organizational missions, mission/business processes, and the
610 systems supporting those missions/processes require an integrated view for managing risk. NIST
611 SP 800-39 provides guidance for an integrated, organization-wide program for managing
612 information security risk. To integrate the risk management process throughout the organization,

613 three levels of risk management are defined: (i) *organization*; (ii) *mission/business processes*;
614 and (iii) *system*. Figure 2 illustrates the organization-wide multi-level risk management
615 structure.

617 **Figure 2: Special Publication 800-39 Multi-Level Risk Management**

618 The three respective levels of cybersecurity risk management described in the Cybersecurity
619 Framework and SP 800-39 are equivalent. The SP 800-39 Levels and roles are referenced
620 throughout the SP 800-37. The equivalence of the Cybersecurity Framework and SP 800-39
621 organizational levels, and the current alignment of SP 800-37 with the SP 800-39 Levels, help to
622 illustrate the alignment of organizational levels across all three RM publications.

623 Additionally, the SP 800-39 provides process and roles for cybersecurity risk management. The
624 Cybersecurity Framework provides a structure for organizing cybersecurity risk management
625 through activities like reconciling cybersecurity requirements.

626 **NIST Risk Management Framework**

627 The organization-wide risk management process of SP 800-39 is central to administering the
628 RMF's six-step process in alignment with business/mission objectives and architectural
629 considerations, as shown in Figure 3.

630
631
Figure 3: Cybersecurity Risk Management Framework described in NIST SP 800-37

632 The RMF provides a method of coordinating the inter-related risk management standards and
633 guidelines described below:

634 • **Federal Information Processing Standards (FIPS) Publication 199,** *Standards for*
635 *Security Categorization of Federal Information and Information Systems,* is a standard
636 for categorizing information and systems based on the potential impact to an
637 organization and its ability to accomplish its mission, protect assets, fulfill its legal
638 responsibilities, and maintain day-to-day functions. FIPS Publication 199 requires
639 federal agencies to categorize their systems as low-impact, moderate-impact, or high-
640 impact for the security objectives of confidentiality, integrity, and availability. Federal
641 agencies use **Special Publication 800-60,** *Guide for Mapping Types of Information*
642 *and Information Systems to Security Categories,* to identify all information types
643 processed, stored, or transmitted by these systems. Each identified information type has
644 an impact value (low, moderate, or high) assigned for each of the security objectives of
645 confidentiality, integrity, and availability.

646 • **FIPS Publication 200,** *Minimum Security Requirements for Federal Information and*
647 *Information Systems,* specifies (i) minimum security requirements for information and
648 systems supporting executive agencies of the federal government and (ii) a risk-based
649 process for selecting the security controls necessary to satisfy the minimum security

650 requirements. This standard promotes the development, implementation, and operation
651 of more secure systems within the federal government by establishing minimal levels of
652 due diligence and facilitates a more consistent, comparable, and repeatable approach for
653 selecting and specifying security controls for systems.

654 • **SP 800-53,** *Security and Privacy Controls for Federal Information Systems and*
655 *Organizations,* provides a comprehensive catalog of security and privacy controls and a
656 process for selecting controls to protect organizational operations, assets, individuals,
657 and other organizations from a diverse set of threats. The controls are customizable and
658 implemented as part of an organization-wide process to manage information security and
659 privacy risk. SP 800-53 also provides a methodology to develop specialized sets of
660 controls, or overlays, tailored for specific types of mission/business functions,
661 technologies, or environments of operation. **SP 800-53A,** *Guide for Assessing the*
662 *Security Controls in Federal Information Systems and Organizations*, provides a set of
663 procedures for conducting assessments of the information security and privacy controls
664 in SP 800-53.

665 • **SP 800-37,** *Guide for Applying the Risk Management Framework to Federal*
666 *Information Systems,* provides guidelines for applying the Risk Management
667 Framework (RMF) to federal systems. The RMF promotes the concept of near real-time
668 risk management and ongoing system authorization through the implementation of
669 robust continuous monitoring processes. It provides senior leaders the information to
670 make risk-based decisions for their systems, integrating information security into
671 enterprise architecture and the system development lifecycle. The document describes
672 how to apply the RMF to systems through a six-step process, including:

673 (i) the categorization of information and systems;

674 (ii) the selection of controls;

675 (iii) the implementation of controls;

676 (iv) the assessment of control effectiveness;

677 (v) the authorization of the system; and

678 (vi) ongoing monitoring of controls and the security state of the system.

679 • **SP 800-137,** *Information Security Continuous Monitoring for Federal Information*
680 *Systems and Organizations,* supports the ongoing monitoring of security controls and
681 the security state of systems. 800-137 provides guidance on developing an agency-wide
682 information security continuous monitoring (ISCM) strategy and implementing an ISCM
683 program. An ISCM program assists federal agencies in making informed risk
684 management decisions by providing ongoing awareness of threats, vulnerabilities, and
685 security control effectiveness.

686

687
688
689
690
691
692
693
694
695
696
697

- **SP 800-39, *Managing Information Security Risk,*** provides guidance for an integrated, organization-wide program for managing information security risk resulting from the operation and use of federal systems. The publication describes a multi-level approach to risk management and applying risk management concepts across an organization. The approach includes three distinct organizational levels[13]: the organization level; the mission/business process level; and the system level. The application of risk management processes among these levels is described in four key steps: "Framing Risk," "Assessing Risk," "Responding to Risk," and "Monitoring Risk." The risk management process is carried out seamlessly across the three levels, with the overall objective of continuous improvement in the organization's risk-related activities and effective communication within and across the three levels.

698
699
700
701
702
703
704
705

- **SP 800-30, *Guide for Conducting Risk Assessments,*** provides guidance for conducting risk assessments of federal systems and organizations. This document provides guidance for carrying out each of the steps in the risk assessment process and how risk assessments and other organizational risk management processes complement and inform each other. SP 800-30 also provides guidance to organizations on identifying specific risk factors to monitor on an ongoing basis. These monitoring activities enable organizations to determine whether risks have increased to unacceptable levels and to implement appropriate risk responses.

706
707
708

Federal agencies use the RMF to "develop, document, and implement an agency-wide program to improve the security of its information and systems that support the operations and assets of the agency.[15]"

709 **The Cybersecurity Framework**

710
711

The three primary components of the Cybersecurity Framework are the **Core**, **Implementation Tiers**, and **Profiles**.

712
713
714
715
716
717
718
719
720
721

One of the central features of the Cybersecurity Framework is its ability to translate highly technical and specialized cybersecurity language to a standardized language that experts outside of cybersecurity can understand. This allows a larger team of experts to participate in cybersecurity risk management dialogs and to incorporate considerations of cybersecurity more broadly as part of how an organization manages its risks . The **Cybersecurity Framework Core** is the structure that enables that translation. Specifically, it provides a set of specific cybersecurity outcomes and reference examples of guidance to achieve those outcomes. The Core is not a checklist of actions to perform; rather, it presents key cybersecurity outcomes identified by industry as helpful in managing cybersecurity risk. The Core itself is composed of four elements: Functions, Categories, Subcategories, and Informative References.

---

[13] SP 800-39 uses the term "Tier." To avoid confusion between the Cybersecurity Framework "Implementation Tiers" and the SP 800-39 organizational Tiers are referred to as "Levels" in this document.

722 The Cybersecurity Framework *Functions* – Identify, Protect, Detect, Respond, and Recover –
723 provide a high level risk management vocabulary that is meaningful to cybersecurity experts and
724 accessible to non-cybersecurity experts. For this reason, the Functions are applicable to both
725 cybersecurity risk management and enterprise risk management, where cybersecurity is
726 considered along with other organizational concerns. As illustrated in the Figure 4, the "bow tie"
727 risk diagram,[14] the five Functions also balance prevention and reaction, including preparatory
728 activities to enable the best possible outcome from that reaction. This balance allows Functions
729 to act as a high level expression of risk management strategy and structure for risk assessment.

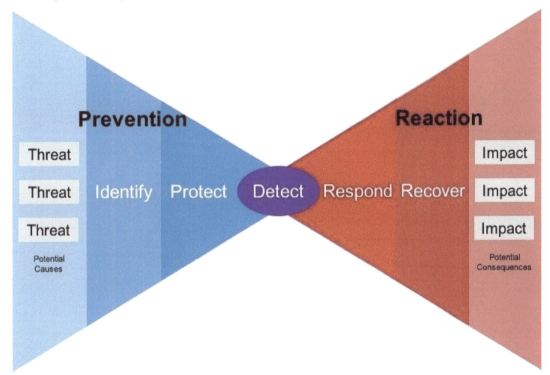

730
731 **Figure 4: Balancing Organizational Focus with Cybersecurity Framework Functions**

732 While Functions are often depicted linearly, the outcomes and dependencies associated with each
733 Function can be iterative and often non-sequential. For example, continuous process
734 improvements and lessons learned from the Respond and Recover Functions can inform the
735 Protect Function. These data may be coupled with new best practices and information sharing
736 from other organizations that also inform federal agency considerations for continuous process
737 improvement in the Prevent Function.

738 The rest of the Cybersecurity Framework Core is subordinate to the Functions, and is composed
739 of Categories, Subcategories, and Informative References. The Core hierarchy depicted in Figure
740 5 ensures a frame of reference. This greatly enriches the context of cybersecurity conversations
741 or documents.

---

[14] Bow tie diagrams are commonly used to represent all hazards, and proactive and reactive measures to address those hazards. This type of visualization may be helpful when considering cybersecurity along side of other enterprise concerns.

Figure 5: The Cybersecurity Framework Core

Categories are the subdivisions of a Function into groups of cybersecurity outcomes closely tied to programmatic needs and particular activities. Examples of Categories include "Asset Management," "Access Control," and "Detection Processes." *Subcategories* further divide a Category into specific outcomes of technical and/or management activities. Each subcategory is supported by one or more *Informative References*, which are specific sections of standards, guidelines, and practices that illustrate a method to achieve the outcomes described.

Using the Core taxonomy of Functions, Categories, and Subcategories, the Cybersecurity Framework fosters communication within and among the levels of an organization. The Cybersecurity Framework provides a common language among the representatives of various units of an organization and between organizations, including partners and suppliers. This helps to align a shared vision of security outcomes.

Another key feature of the Cybersecurity Framework is the qualitative measurement of organizational risk practices or behaviors. This allows organizations to identify their desirable behaviors, measure current behaviors, determine gaps, and work to improve.

The **Cybersecurity Framework Implementation Tiers** provide a method for organizations to view cybersecurity risk behaviors and the processes for managing risk. The Implementation Tiers range from Partial (Tier 1) to Adaptive (Tier 4) and describe an increasing degree of rigor and sophistication in cybersecurity risk management practices. They also describe the extent to which cybersecurity risk management is informed by business needs and is integrated into an organization's overall risk management practices. The Cybersecurity Framework characterizes three distinct cybersecurity risk management practices:

765   • *Risk Management Process* – a reflection of cybersecurity risk management within an
766   organization.

767   • *Integrated Risk Management Program* – the consideration of cybersecurity alongside of
768   other organizational concerns.

769   • *External Participation* – The bi-directional flow and consideration of information to
770   better organizational Risk Management Process and Integrated Risk Management
771   Program, as well as the Risk Management Processes and Integrated Risk Management
772   Programs of other organizations.

773   While organizations identified as Implementation Tier 1 (Partial) are encouraged to consider
774   moving toward Implementation Tier 2 or greater, *Implementation Tiers do not represent maturity*
775   *levels.* Progression to higher Implementation Tiers is encouraged when the reduction in
776   cybersecurity risk is deemed to be appropriate and cost-effective.

777   **Cybersecurity Framework Profiles** can be used to describe the current state and/or the desired
778   target state of specific cybersecurity activities. They enable users to draw upon the Framework
779   Core outcomes, while supporting ways to customize those outcomes to organization-specific
780   missions, regulatory requirements, and operating environments. Profiles support
781   business/mission requirements and aid in communicating risk within and between organizations.
782   *Current Profiles* indicate the cybersecurity outcomes that are now being achieved. *Target*
783   *Profiles* indicate the outcomes needed to achieve the desired cybersecurity risk management
784   goals.

785   Comparison of Current and Target Profiles may reveal gaps and corresponding improvements
786   needed to meet cybersecurity risk management objectives. The organization's business needs and
787   risk management processes drive a mitigation priority for gaps. This risk-based approach enables
788   an organization to estimate resources needed (e.g., staffing, funding) to set cybersecurity goals
789   that can be achieved in a cost-effective, prioritized manner.

790   Figure 6 depicts Business/Process personnel within an organization evaluating Profile gaps,
791   prioritizing the sequence of gap mitigation, determining mitigation resources, and coordinating
792   mitigation with Implementation/Operations level personnel. In all instances, the central artifacts
793   and work products are Profiles.

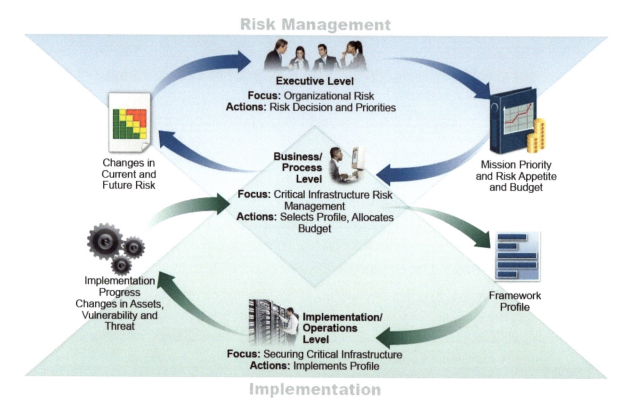

794
795   Figure 6: Notional Information and Decision Flows within an Organization

796 **Appendix B—Acronyms**

797 Selected acronyms and abbreviations used in this paper are defined below.
798

AO	Authorizing Official
CI	Critical Infrastructure
CISO	Chief Information Security Officer
EO	Executive Order
FIPS	Federal Information Processing Standards
FISMA	Federal Information Security Management Act of 2002, as amended
HIPAA	Health Insurance Portability and Accountability Act
HVA	High Value Asset
ISCM	Information Security Continuous Monitoring
ISO	International Organization for Standardization
ITL	Information Technology Laboratory
NIST	National Institute of Standards and Technology
OMB	Office of Management and Budget
POA&M	Plan of Action and Milestones
RFC	Request for Comment
RFI	Request for Information
RMF	Risk Management Framework
SAR	Security Assessment Report
SP	Special Publication
SSP	System Security Plan

799

800 **Appendix C—Glossary**

Agency	See *Executive Agency*
Chief Information Officer [PL 104-106, Sec. 5125(b)]	Agency official responsible for:
	(i) Providing advice and other assistance to the head of the executive agency and other senior management personnel of the agency to ensure that information technology is acquired and information resources are managed in a manner that is consistent with laws, Executive Orders, directives, policies, regulations, and priorities established by the head of the agency;
	(ii) Developing, maintaining, and facilitating the implementation of a sound and integrated information technology architecture for the agency; and
	(iii) Promoting the effective and efficient design and operation of all major information resources management processes for the agency, including improvements to work processes of the agency.
Chief Information Security Officer	See *Senior Agency Information Security Officer*
Common Control [NIST SP 800-37]	A security control that is inherited by one or more organizational information systems. See *Security Control Inheritance*.
Common Control Provider [NIST SP 800-37]	An organizational official responsible for the development, implementation, assessment, and monitoring of common controls (i.e., security controls inherited by information systems).
Cybersecurity [CNSSI 4009]	The ability to protect or defend the use of cyberspace from cyber attacks.
Enterprise [CNSSI 4009]	An organization with a defined mission/goal and a defined boundary, using information systems to execute that mission, and with responsibility for managing its own risks and performance. An enterprise may consist of all or some of the following business aspects: acquisition, program management, financial management (e.g., budgets), human resources, security, and information systems, information and mission management. See *Organization*.
Executive Agency [41 U.S.C., Sec. 403]	An executive department specified in 5 United States Code (U.S.C.), Sec. 101; a military department specified in 5 U.S.C., Sec. 102; an independent establishment as defined in 5 U.S.C., Sec. 104(1); and a wholly owned government corporation fully subject to the provisions of 31 U.S.C., Chapter 91.

Federal Agency	See *Executive Agency*
Federal Information System [40 U.S.C., Sec. 11331]	An information system used or operated by an executive agency, by a contractor of an executive agency, or by another organization on behalf of an executive agency.
High Value Asset [OMB M-17-09]	Those assets, federal information systems, information, and data for which an unauthorized access, use, disclosure, disruption, modification, or destruction could cause a significant impact to the United States' national security interests, foreign relations, economy – or to the public confidence, civil liberties, or public health and safety of the American people.
Hybrid Security Control [NIST SP 800-53]	A security control that is implemented in an information system in part as a common control and in part as a system-specific control. See *Common Control* and *System-Specific Security Control*.
Information [CNSSI 4009] [FIPS 199]	Any communication or representation of knowledge such as facts, data, or opinions in any medium or form, including textual, numerical, graphic, cartographic, narrative, or audiovisual. An instance of an information type.
Information Security [44 U.S.C., Sec 3541]	The protection of information and information systems from unauthorized access, use, disclosure, disruption, modification, or destruction in order to provide confidentiality, integrity, and availability.
Information System [44 U.S.C., Sec 3502]	A discrete set of information resources organized for the collection, processing, maintenance, use, sharing, dissemination, or disposition of information.
Information System Security Officer	Individual assigned responsibility by the senior agency information security officer, authorizing official, management official, or information system owner for ensuring that the appropriate operational security posture is maintained for an information system or program.

Information Technology [40 U.S.C., Sec. 1401]	Any equipment or interconnected system or subsystem of equipment that is used in the automatic acquisition, storage, manipulation, management, movement, control, display, switching, interchange, transmission, or reception of data or information by the executive agency. For purposes of the preceding sentence, equipment is used by an executive agency if the equipment is used by the executive agency directly or is used by a contractor under a contract with the executive agency which: (i) requires the use of such equipment; or (ii) requires the use, to a significant extent, of such equipment in the performance of a service or the furnishing of a product. The term information technology includes computers, ancillary equipment, software, firmware, and similar procedures, services (including support services), and related resources.
Information Type [FIPS 199]	A specific category of information (e.g., privacy, medical, proprietary, financial, investigative, contractor sensitive, security management) defined by an organization or in some instances, by a specific law, Executive Order, directive, policy, or regulation.
Organization [FIPS 200, Adapted]	An entity of any size, complexity, or positioning within an organizational structure (e.g., a federal agency or, as appropriate, any of its operational elements). See *Enterprise*.
Plan of Action and Milestones or POA&M [OMB Memorandum 02-01]	A document that identifies tasks needing to be accomplished. It details resources required to accomplish the elements of the plan, any milestones in meeting the tasks, and scheduled completion dates for the milestones.
Risk [CNSSI 4009]	A measure of the extent to which an entity is threatened by a potential circumstance or event, and typically a function of: (i) the adverse impacts that would arise if the circumstance or event occurs; and (ii) the likelihood of occurrence. [Note: Information system-related security risks are those risks that arise from the loss of confidentiality, integrity, or availability of information or information systems and reflect the potential adverse impacts to organizational operations (including mission, functions, image, or reputation), organizational assets, individuals, other organizations, and the Nation.]

Risk Executive (Function) [CNSSI 4009]	An individual or group within an organization that helps to ensure that:
	(i) security risk -related considerations for individual information systems, to include the authorization decisions for those systems, are viewed from an organization-wide perspective with regard to the overall strategic goals and objectives of the organization in carrying out its missions and business functions; and
	(ii) managing risk from individual information systems is consistent across the organization, reflects organizational risk tolerance, and is considered along with other organizational risks affecting mission/business success.
Risk Management [CNSSI 4009, adapted]	The program and supporting processes to manage information security risk to organizational operations (including mission, functions, image, reputation), organizational assets, individuals, other organizations, and the Nation, and includes:
	(i) establishing the context for risk-related activities;
	(ii) assessing risk;
	(iii) responding to risk once determined; and
	(iv) monitoring risk over time.
Risk Register	A central record of current risks for a given scope or organization. Current risks are comprised of both accepted risks and risk that are have a planned mitigation path (i.e., risks to-be-eliminated as annotated in a POA&M)
Security Categorization	The process of determining the security category for information or an information system. Security categorization methodologies are described in CNSS Instruction 1253 for national security systems and in FIPS 199 for other than national security systems.
Security Control Inheritance [CNSSI 4009]	A situation in which an information system or application receives protection from security controls (or portions of security controls) that are developed, implemented, assessed, authorized, and monitored by entities other than those responsible for the system or application; entities either internal or external to the organization where the system or application resides. See *Common Control*.
Security Controls [FIPS 199, CNSSI 4009]	The management, operational, and technical controls (i.e., safeguards or countermeasures) prescribed for an information system to protect the confidentiality, integrity, and availability of the system and its information.

Security Plan [NIST SP 800-18]	Formal document that provides an overview of the security requirements for an information system or an information security program and describes the security controls in place or planned for meeting those requirements. See *System Security Plan.*
Senior Agency Information Security Officer [44 U.S.C., Sec. 3544]	Official responsible for carrying out the Chief Information Officer responsibilities under FISMA and serving as the Chief Information Officer's primary liaison to the agency's authorizing officials, information system owners, and information system security officers. [Note: Organizations subordinate to federal agencies may use the term *Senior Information Security Officer* or *Chief Information Security Officer* to denote individuals filling positions with similar responsibilities to Senior Agency Information Security Officers.]
System	See *Information System*
System Security Plan [NIST SP 800-18]	Formal document that provides an overview of the security requirements for an information system and describes the security controls in place or planned for meeting those requirements.
System-Specific Security Control [NIST SP 800-37]	A security control for an information system that has not been designated as a common control or the portion of a hybrid control that is to be implemented within an information system.
Tailoring [NIST SP 800-53, CNSSI 4009]	The process by which a security control baseline is modified based on: (i) the application of scoping guidance; (ii) the specification of compensating security controls, if needed; and (iii) the specification of organization-defined parameters in the security controls via explicit assignment and selection statements.
Threat [CNSSI 4009]	Any circumstance or event with the potential to adversely impact organizational operations (including mission, functions, image, or reputation), organizational assets, individuals, other organizations, or the Nation through an information system via unauthorized access, destruction, disclosure, modification of information, and/or denial of service.

801

802
Appendix D—References

[1]   Federal Information Security Modernization Act of 2014, Pub. L. 107-347 (Title III), 116 Stat 2946. https://www.gpo.gov/fdsys/pkg/PLAW-113publ283/pdf/PLAW-113publ283.pdf

[2]   Federal Information Security Management Act of 2002, Pub. L. 107-347 (Title III), 116 Stat 2946. https://www.gpo.gov/fdsys/pkg/PLAW-107publ347/pdf/PLAW-107publ347.pdf.

[3]   Joint Task Force Transformation Initiative, *Managing Information Security Risk: Organization, Mission, and Information System View*, NIST Special Publication (SP) 800-39, March 2011. http://dx.doi.org/10.6028/NIST.SP.800-39

[4]   Joint Task Force Transformation Initiative, *Guide for Applying the Risk Management Framework to Federal Information Systems: A Security Life Cycle Approach*, NIST Special Publication (SP) 800-37 Revision 1, February 2010. http://dx.doi.org/10.6028/NIST.SP.800-37r1

[5]   National Institute of Standards and Technology (NIST), *Framework for Improving Critical Infrastructure Cybersecurity,* Version 1.0, February 12, 2014. https://www.nist.gov/sites/default/files/documents/cyberframework/cybersecurity-framework-021214.pdf

[6]   Executive Order no. 13636, *Improving Critical Infrastructure Cybersecurity*, DCPD-201300091, February 12, 2013. http://www.gpo.gov/fdsys/pkg/FR-2013-02-19/pdf/2013-03915.pdf

[7]   Cybersecurity Enhancement Act of 2014, Pub. L. 113-274. https://www.gpo.gov/fdsys/pkg/PLAW-113publ274/pdf/PLAW-113publ274.pdf

[8]   Office of Management and Budget (OMB), *Fiscal Year2013 Reporting Instructions for the Federal Information Security Management Act and Agency Privacy Management,* OMB Memorandum 14-04, November 18, 2013. https://obamawhitehouse.archives.gov/sites/default/files/omb/memoranda/2014/m-14-04.pdf

[9]   The White House, Circular A-130, *Managing Federal Information as a Strategic Resource*, July 2016. https://www.whitehouse.gov/sites/default/files/omb/assets/OMB/circulars/a130/a130revis ed.pdf

[10]   U.S. Department of Commerce, *Standards for Security Categorization of Federal Information and Information Systems,* Federal Information Processing Standards (FIPS) Publication 199, February 2004. http://dx.doi.org/10.6028/NIST.FIPS.199

[11]   K. Stine, R. Kissel, C. Barker, J. Fahlsing, J. Gulick, *Guide for Mapping Types of Information and Information Systems to Security Categories*, NIST

Special Publication (SP) 800-60, Revision 1, August 2008.
http://dx.doi.org/10.6028/NIST.SP.800-60v1r1

[12]   U.S. Department of Commerce, *Minimum Security Requirements for Federal
         Information and Information Systems,* Federal Information Processing
         Standards (FIPS) Publication 200, March 2006.
         http://dx.doi.org/10.6028/NIST.FIPS.200

[13]   Joint Task Force Transformation Initiative, *Security and Privacy Controls
         for Federal Information Systems and Organizations,* NIST Special
         Publication (SP) 800-53 Revision 4, April 2013.
         http://dx.doi.org/10.6028/NIST.SP.800-53r4

[14]   Joint Task Force Transformation Initiative, *Assessing Security and Privacy
         Controls in Federal Information Systems and Organizations,* NIST Special
         Publication (SP) 800-53A Revision 4, December 2014.
         http://dx.doi.org/10.6028/NIST.SP.800-53Ar4

[15]   K. Dempsey, N. Chawla, A. Johnson, R. Johnston, A. Jones, A. Orebaugh,
         M. Scholl, K. Stine, *Information Security Continuous Monitoring (ISCM) for
         Federal Information Systems and Organizations,* NIST Special Publication
         (SP) 800-137, September 2011. http://dx.doi.org/10.6028/NIST.SP.800-137

[16]   Joint Task Force Transformation Initiative, *Guide for Conducting Risk
         Assessments,* NIST Special Publication (SP) 800-30 Revision 1, September
         2012. http://dx.doi.org/10.6028/NIST.SP.800-30r1

[17]   J. Boyens, C. Paulsen, R. Moorthy, N. Bartol, *Supply Chain Risk
         Management Practices for Federal Information Systems and Organizations,*
         NIST Special Publication (SP) 800-161, April 2015.
         http://dx.doi.org/10.6028/NIST.SP.800-161

[18]   R. Ross, P. Viscuso, G. Guissanie, K. Dempsey, M. Riddle, *Protecting
         Controlled Unclassified Information in Nonfederal Information Systems and
         Organizations,* NIST Special Publication (SP) 800-171, June 2015.
         http://dx.doi.org/10.6028/NIST.SP.800-171

[19]   International Organization for Standardization/International Electrotechnical
         Commission, *Information technology – Security techniques – Information
         security management systems,* ISO/IEC 27001:2013, September 2013.
         https://www.iso.org/standard/54534.html [accessed on 3/10/17]

[20]   Information Systems Audit and Control Association (ISACA), Control
         Objectives for Information and Related Technology (COBIT) version 5
         [Web site], https://www.isaca.org/cobit [accessed on 3/10/17].

[22]   Office of Management and Budget (OMB), *Cybersecurity Strategy and
         Implementation Plan for the Federal Civilian Government,* OMB
         Memorandum 16-04, October 30, 2015.
         https://obamawhitehouse.archives.gov/sites/default/files/omb/memoranda/20
         16/m-16-04.pdf

803